Which planet is closest to the Sun?

Mercury

Mercury is a small planet.

Which planet is next to Mercury?

Venus

Venus is a rocky planet.

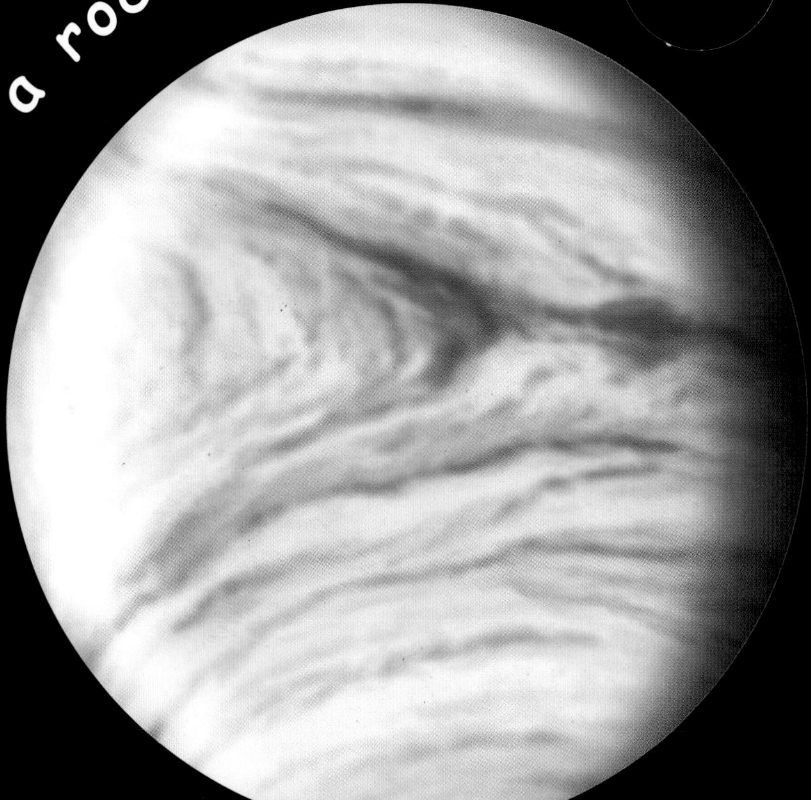

Which planet is next to Venus?

Earth

We live on planet Earth.

Which planet is next to Earth?

Mars

Mars is a red planet.

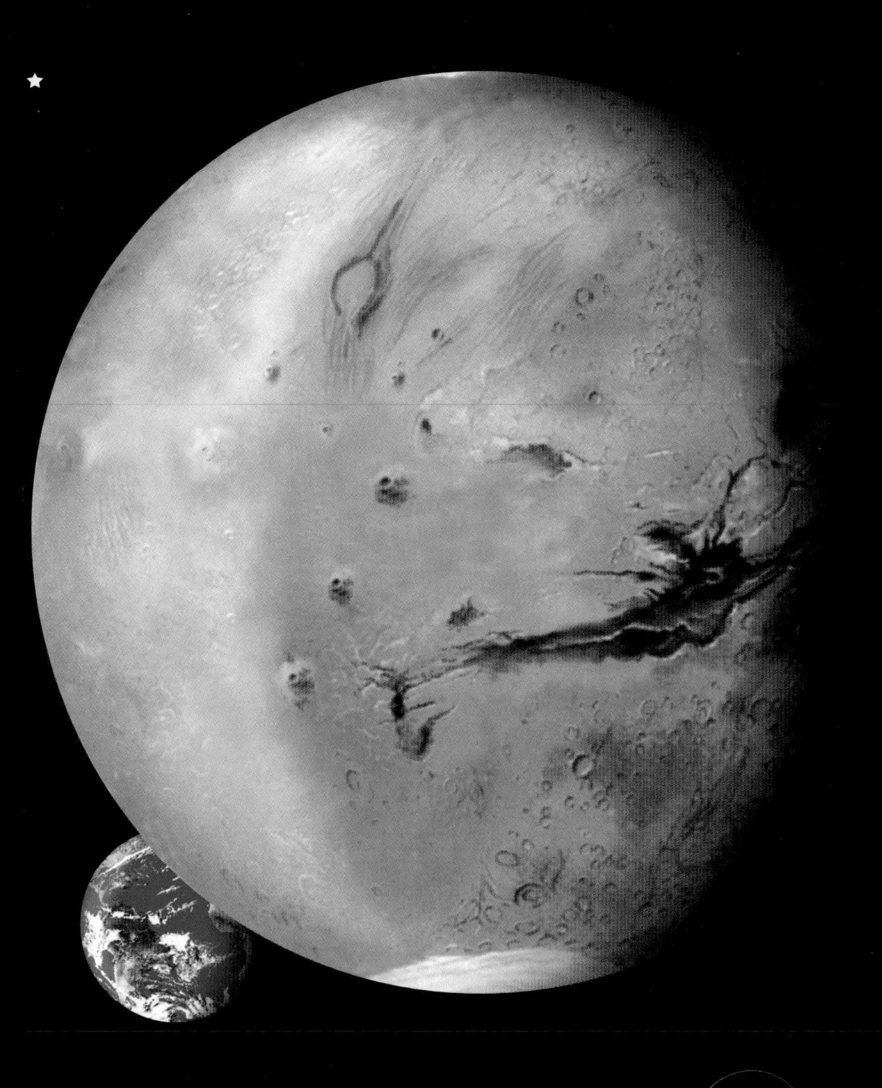

Which planet is next to Mars?

Jupiter

Jupiter is a big planet.

Which planet is next to Saturn?

Uranus

Uranus is a green planet.

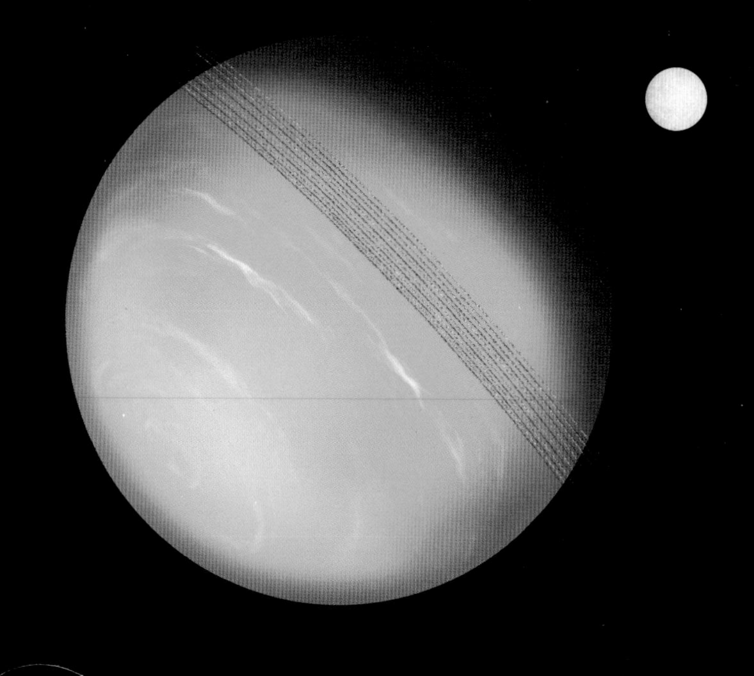

xt to Uranus?

Nept

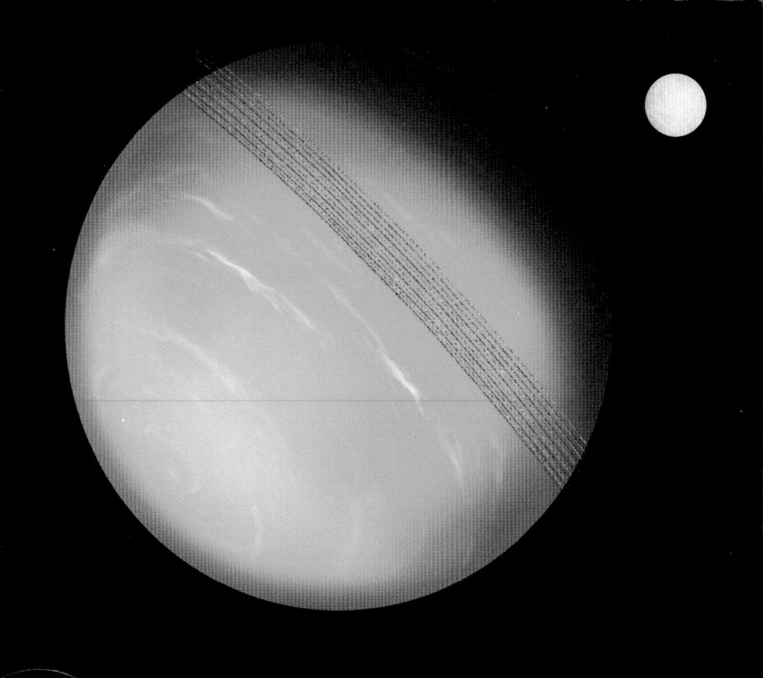

xt to Uranus?

Nept